Little Bit

Patricia Lovell

Dedication

I dedicate this book to children everywhere
and to the inner child in every adult.

Acknowledgements

Lots of Little Bits have come together to help bring this book to fruition. Thank you doesn't seem a big enough word to thank all the other Bits that encouraged me and believed in Little Bit.
Those wonderful Bits include my husband Brian (my greatest fan).
Joanne Russell who was the first to say that
Little Bit was a story that 'must be shared.'

Vivienne Cooper who immediately visualised the first story as a book a thought that hadn't even entered my head. Lynne Luxton who received each Little Bit, bit by bit always giving me insightful feedback.

My grateful thanks go to Di Collins the most enthusiastic typist I have ever met. I am the fortunate one that our paths continue to cross. Another grateful and big thanks to Artist Lennie Robson who jumped on board and brought Little Bit into the wonderful world of colour it was as though she could see inside my head
as she bought my vision alive.

Last but not least a big thankyou to my publisher Karen McDermott for believing that Little Bit needs to be shared and
seen by lots of other bits.
Thanks also to my editor Dannielle Line for assuring Little Bit's clarity.

To you all I send love from my heart to yours and
the biggest smile I can muster.

Contents

Chapter 1: Little Bit   1

Chapter 2: A Little Bit More   5

Chapter 3: A Little Bit of Time   9

Chapter 4: A Little Bit of Thought   13

Chapter 5: A Little Bit Sceptic   19

Chapter 6: A Little Bit of Fear   25

Chapter 7: A Little Bit of Faith   31

1
Little Bit

Little Bit knew itself as love and complete.

Little Bit observed all the Bits around enjoying being themselves too. No one judged another.

Then into this space came the thoughts of Us and Them. The Ego arrived, and like a Virus, infected all the Bits, who compared, competed and controlled them from within and then they projected that onto another and another.

Fear arrived also, competing with the Love, and Fear became stronger and stronger. The Ego's Fear made all the Bits doubt and not feel good enough or have enough, filling them with thoughts of getting more, so they could then feel good about themselves.

All the affected Bits were finding their own way to feel better about themselves. Some tried to make others feel bad so they could feel better. Others hurt themselves by withdrawing, because no one could hurt as much as they could. All this Fear grew and looked more real than the Love.

So many dark things, and blaming themselves, or others, or thinking, 'I am right, and they are wrong.'

They were always trying to be more and have more.

Until Mother Earth made a shift. The energies were changing. Little Bit felt it. Some Bits felt it and some Bits didn't.

Those that could feel it realised with the energy came a great light. That powerful light brought the darkness the Fear and the Ego created into the light to see and feel, not to hurt, but to put a stop to seeing it as real.

This darkness manifested in so many ways for all the Bits.

Anger, blame, shame, resentments, judgements, controlling behaviours, abusing others or staying the victim, and so much more, were all brought into the light.

As more and more Bits woke up, they realised they couldn't deny the pain of what believing in the Ego and the Fear did.

They knew they must embrace it. Some wallowed, some didn't, and some remembered their original self-love.

When they remembered love, they could then forgive themselves and others if they needed to.

One amazing thing for Little Bit was that Little Bit realised the pain they were experiencing was the pain of separation from their original self and from the Divine Creative Source.

So, Bit by Bit made their way into the light energy, able to love all that fear created. To name them, thank them, and set them free. Little Bit could simply 'be' again, to observe others again, not with any thoughts of comparing, competing or controlling, but through their original eyes of Love. To remember they were all Bits together making a whole.

Remembering also, as they healed, their healing would help and bring healing to the whole, and that would always be enough.

2
A Little Bit More

Little Bit felt so light-hearted and could see that light in so many other Little Bits. It was as though they'd all arrived in a happy place.

It felt good.

Little Bit though, could still see others who only absorbed a part of the light. That didn't feel right or wrong. It was just how it was.

Still, Little Bit felt excited there would be a gathering, a getting together where more remembering took place with some other Bits.

For Little Bit sometimes still struggled with the challenges, especially from those that retained some darkness from the Virus to overcome.

This part of the Virus also had a name, Expectation. Little Bit observed how the colours changed in those Bits that expected everyone to know what they wanted. Or how they wished to be noticed, included or to give them what they wanted.

When nothing happened how they expected, the weight of their Expectations made them topple over.

That weight made them stay down or get angry, be mean or think there was so much wrong with them. How could any others love them or acknowledge them?

Little Bit pondered without judgement on how to help.

Little Bit came up with an idea to remind them about the effects of the Virus. To remind them the Virus wasn't them. To remind them they had a Voice and they could use their Voice to say what was best for them. And to say when something didn't feel ok. Or best of all, to use their Voice to say what they would like to do. Plus, listen to the Voice inside their heads. The Voice that fills them with joy, not the one that tells them there is something wrong with them or that they deserve to be unhappy. That's the Voice of the Virus, not the Voice of their real loving self.

Then Little Bit smiled, and everyone felt the power of the Smile.

Those already in a happy place felt even more joyous, and those making their way to a happier place felt lighter and lighter.

Lighting up the memories of their original loving selves.

A Smile is like medicine whenever a part of the Virus creeps in.

A Smile will always help all the Bits to remember the goodness in every Bit.

3
A Little Bit of Time

Little Bit was walking along a beautiful track through the trees, gazing at and breathing in the colours of the wildflowers. Little Bit felt the warmth of the sun and the freshness of the air.

Little Bit noticed all of this with a full and grateful heart. Also feeling grateful for the past passage of time that helped Little Bit remember to take, and to have these moments of joy.

Little Bit was also recalling how difficult recent times had been.

Another part of the Virus struck not only Little Bit, but so many other Bits. It was as though they'd all been turned upside down and shaken about by Time.

There was rushing here and there, and the greater the rushing, the more forgetting. Forgetting what they were doing, where they put things. Some even broke things in their rush and forgot to smile at the other Bits around them.

Time struck.

Little Bit's light dimmed along with the other Bits.

What to do?

Little Bit, in the middle of this craziness, had a lightbulb moment. Little Bit followed up on this idea and went off to meet and talk with the Wise Bit, who didn't seem affected by this part of the Virus at all. Little Bit supposed that was why Wise Bit was called Wise.

Wise Bit asked Little Bit to look into all the Bits' colours. Really look.

So Little Bit looked and spotted some swirls of Fear like a fine mist. So fine, that all the Bits stopped noticing it. This mist was lighter in some and darker in others. Whatever the shade, it blurred what is real and what isn't real. The mist made all the Bits victims of Time.

They were thinking there wasn't enough time, or they had to catch up. When Bits have those thoughts, the rushing begins. The Fear of not being able to perform well or keep up brought back the comparing, competing and control.

With a gentle Smile, Wise Bit said, "All this because a mist covered the Truth. This Truth being that the sun rises in the morning and sets in the evening. All the moments in between and after the sun sets are moments all the Bits can structure for themselves. Do all they need to do, bit by bit. Moments fill the space of the day so there's no need to crowd each moment and the Bits get to choose how to use the moments. Time is like a circle and all the Bits can continue to flow in their own circle. The circle each Bit lives in flows to their own choices."

Wise Bit smiled again and said, "So choose how to use your time Wisely. Let it work for you, not against you as time simply flows. Time doesn't do anything. It's what all the Bits do with it. Look to Time as a friend, not the Fear of Time."

Wise Bit asked Little Bit to remind all the Bits to laugh at themselves, to shake with laughter. For when Fear is disguised as Time, the rushing makes things seem longer through having to go back fixing mistakes or cleaning up messes. While slowing down, Time can seem faster as the things you wish to do and get done goes smoothly. With a steady pace, your Light and Love shines through.

While walking, Little Bit pondered on all of Wise Bit's words, recalling Wise Bit's reminder to breathe. To take deep breaths, to slow thoughts down.

Little Bit smiled, looking around again at the trees, the flowers and the sky. Little Bit breathed deeply, enjoying that moment and the next moment, feeling the Love and Light that was real inside of Little Bit, flowing smoothly and brightly.

Little Bit was not only grateful, but content.

4
A Little Bit of Thought

Little Bit set off for a planned walk to the park with a small bag of food suitable for the ducks that spend their day seemingly effortlessly gliding across the pond. It was one of Little Bit's favourite places. Though Little Bit knew that the gliding took effort with the ducks' webbed feet working away below the surface of the pond.

Before feeding the ducks, Little Bit sat awhile happily watching toddler Bits having fun by the pond's edge.

Little Bit laughed when one almost toppled in. The laugh then turned to a stab-like pain in Little Bit's heart as the thoughts crowded in about how unpleasant that may have been for the toddler.

Little Bit had been Thoughtless.

Little Bit felt more memories of Thoughtlessness arise.

Times when Little Bit said the wrong thing even without meaning to or did something that wasn't nice or thought mean thoughts about another.

Little Bit always felt sorry about those times and said so or tried to do something nice for another.

Because Little Bit always tried to be good, the times when that didn't happen felt so painful, that Little Bit's heart and stomach ached.

These moments of Thoughtlessness weighed so heavily, Little Bit felt worthless. This was a part of the Virus that belonged only to Little Bit.

Another Voice turned up in Little Bit's head, one that felt angry and justified saying, "But what about all those other Bits that do and say mean things to others? They carry on as they are right all the time. They don't even try to be nice."

Little Bit felt the energy surge through, but then realised it didn't feel comfortable. That wasn't Little Bit.

Then another Voice turned up, almost chanting, "Why are they like that? Why are they mean? Why more Whys?"

Little Bit felt the darkness of all these Thoughts swirling around.

A Voice next to, not from inside, spoke gently to Little Bit. Turning to the Voice, Little Bit noticed the Compassion with no judgements pouring from the eyes of the Thoughtful Bit.

Little Bit couldn't look away from those beautiful sparkling eyes and couldn't help holding on to a breath.

Thoughtful reminded Little Bit to breathe again. Then reminded Little Bit, "It's in the darkness that all the Bits can see the Light, and what that Light means is different for each of them. The unreal always appearing as real."

Thoughtful explained the pain of Thoughtlessness is created from feeling less than how you wish to be for yourself and how you wish to act towards other Bits.

The pain feels like you have failed somehow.

"Yes, Little Bit," Thoughtful said, "I heard all your thoughts."

Then Thoughtful mentioned being Thoughtful is to be full of Compassion for yourself first and then others.

"Now let's talk about those Why's," Thoughtful said. "Why is a word that hurts only you, Little Bit."

"How is a word that can bring you back to the Light. When you notice others being mean, you only see them being mean. You don't know their story or what is hurting them. You can only know that if they share their stories. While you can't change that, you can be in charge of how you respond and how you use your words. There's that How again. How is the way you keep coming back to remembering your own Light."

As Little Bit was listening so deeply to what Thoughtful was saying, Thoughtful took Little Bit back to feeling that pain and worthlessness. Not to hurt Little Bit, but to show how real it really was.

Thoughtful guided Little Bit to breathe past these feelings into knowing that sometimes we experience all these painful things that aren't real. They are part of the Virus. Then to breathe back into what is truly Real about yourself and all the Bits.

"Look through the mists of dark thoughts to see your beautiful Light again. Look at the ducks. You see them gliding and think of it as hard work as their webbed feet pedal away to keep them going. Perhaps it helps to look at it this way. They float along and keep working things out as they move along. They appear to enjoy how they go. Now Little Bit, be a bit duck-like. Be calm, smooth and light and work out what is Real and what isn't Real for you as you go along."

Little Bit took a deep, cleansing breath, feeling light again and followed through on the advice of the Thoughtful Bit.

"Go feed the ducks with a smile on your face, breathe deeply and allow Compassion to fill your heart."

That's just what Little Bit did, and at the same time, it felt like Little Bit was gliding along too.

Little Bit was feeling up one minute and down the next, just like a roller coaster soaring to the heights, coming down into the dips, then up again.

Little Bit wished to stay in the Happy Place. These fast descents in the dips made Little Bit doubt the original Loving Self all the Bits really were.

'Some parts of the Virus can't be that bad,' Little Bit thought, and wanted to **forget** all about it. Little Bit wanted to take back control. To make things happen rather than wait for them to happen.

Little Bit plodded along in what felt like heavy shoes to a field taken over by a circus.

Bright colours and movement were everywhere. Little Bit looked at the brightly dressed Bits happily cleaning all the travel dust from the ticket booth and all the painted wagons. They were smiling, laughing and singing out words of encouragement to one another. Watching them was like watching a dance. A well-practiced, dust-cleaning dance.

Feeling brave, Little Bit peeked inside the enormous tent. There was a lot happening inside too. Some Bits were swinging high in the air. Others threw so many things in the air, not dropping anything. Some peddled one-wheel cycles, clowns were on stilts and others were breathing fire. There was a feeling of happiness in the air as the practicing continued.

Little Bit decided this was the place to be where one could pretend highs and lows didn't exist, and the Virus in all its disguises wasn't even true. Being a Sceptic felt good.

Little Bit found an empty seat to sit in and stared in amazement at all that was happening.

Little Bit was so absorbed that a movement right next to Little Bit went unnoticed until a flower was waved in front of Little Bit, followed by a squirt of water. Turning to the source of annoyance, Little Bit's eyes grew bigger, taking in the Clown with a sad, painted face, yet a face that looked like it could smile any minute. That was a bit confusing.

"Why so sad a face?" asked Little Bit.

"Ahhh," the Clown said. "You looked and saw sadness, but what if you looked in another moment and saw happiness?"

Now Little Bit was more confused.

The Clown was quiet for a moment, then explained. "When you first looked at me, you saw sadness. Look inside how you were feeling before you came to the field. The colour and the excitement of the circus distracted you for a moment until you saw your confusion and sadness reflected in my face."

Little Bit didn't want to feel sad, didn't wish to think about any of the reasons for being sad. Little Bit was simply fed up and said so.

The Clown had so much patience allowing Little Bit to vent all these frustrations. After a while, the Clown shared with Little Bit. "Being a sceptic is ok. Being fed up is ok. Being sad is ok. Whatever you feel is ok."

Little Bit, who a moment before felt like being left alone, stayed and listen to the Clown.

"Little Bit," the Clown said, "you have been learning so much, growing in understanding of what is right and true for you and what isn't. Now you are experiencing your impatience. You're getting impatient because there are still parts of the Virus to acknowledge. You set out to learn and all you are feeling is teaching you. Think of the sadness and frustrations as travel dust settling on you. This dust isn't really a part of you. You have simply carried it around. Be patient. Now look at the layers of dust. Picture what they look like. Sadness and frustration can be friends who settle on you as guides to show you that sometimes you are not believing in your Real Self. Being a Sceptic can guide you to what is right for you alone. It may differ from what is right for other Bits, and that's ok too."

The Clown looked at Little Bit. "Once you notice and name the dust, you can blow it away. Becoming a happy cleaner takes practice. Practice on every layer of dust that settles on you now and in the future. Little Bit, all the performers here at the circus have to practice and practice. When their practice and performances are over, they put their feet on the ground and know they did their best."

Little Bit thought about all the things that Little Bit could practice until they not only felt real, they would become Real.

The Clown was glad Little Bit was looking through all those frustrations and seeing all the untruths and disappointments. They were so easy to believe in as they took less practice.

The Clown had some final words for Little Bit.

"Have patience for the Truth to grow so strongly inside you that you will believe in it always. The roller coaster ride is just a way of getting back to where you started. The true you is love, compassion, joyful, kind, thoughtful and patient and so much more. Little Bit, let how you feel guide you and enjoy the roller coaster ride as it moves along its tracks. Keep your feet on the ground whether you are flying high or in a dip. Be patient, the tracks will smooth out."

Little Bit left the circus feeling like weights had been lifted away. Walking felt lighter and Little Bit knew each step reconnected Little Bit to what is True again.

Little Bit resolved to be the best that Little Bit could be, knowing however Little Bit felt, didn't change what is Real and True. To believe and practice believing was enough.

6
A Little Bit of Fear

Little Bit was focusing on overcoming fears and took a ride in a hot air balloon. Little Bit was feeling afraid but not sure why.

Arriving early for the booked ride, Little Bit was looking up at the sky watching a few hot air balloons in the distance.

While looking up, a startling, shimmering energy floated right in front of Little Bit. It wasn't until the energy spoke that Little Bit paid attention.

"Hello Little Bit. Are you looking forward to going up in the sky?"

"Not really," Little Bit truthfully replied. Then asked, "Who are you?"

"I am Fear," the voice of the energy said. "What do I look like to you?"

Little Bit looked hard and only saw a misty shape. "But I can see right through you and I can put my hand through you too." This astounded Little Bit as Fear never felt very comfortable at all. In fact, Little Bit was remembering when Little Bit had to speak up and say something that Little Bit didn't think another Bit would like to hear. Little Bit shook inside and spoke with a shaky voice at those times.

Little Bit was reliving other times when Little Bit had to say no and how sick inside Little Bit felt because that wasn't pleasing to another Bit.

Little Bit was also remembering when it felt like Little Bit couldn't get anything right.

Fear was listening to Little Bit's thoughts and asked Little Bit, "Besides feeling sick, how else did you feel?"

Little Bit didn't have to think long about it saying, "Oh, so tired and weak."

Fear asked Little Bit to look at Fear itself again and asked again, "How do I look to you now?"

"Like nothing," replied Little Bit.

"What did I look like when you were feeling sick in your stomach and weak in your body?" Fear asked.

Little Bit remembered how Fear felt like a dark and heavy cloud. A cloud so dense it was hard to glimpse any light at all.

Fear asked Little Bit to think about Little Bit's greatest fear. "What is it you really fear, Little Bit?"

Little Bits' eyes welled up. Tears spilled out, and it felt like Little Bit's heart was breaking as Little Bit owned the Fear and said, "It's that I am unlovable, and no one will love me."

"Look at me again, Little Bit. What do I look like now?" Fear asked.

"Really Dark in the shape of a shattered heart," Little Bit replied.

"Little Bit, I know you are feeling great pain at present, but will you listen to what I have to say?" Fear asked.

Fear explained, "Little Bit, a moment ago you could see right through me. I didn't really exist. I became what you made me. You give me substance, colour and shape. You gave me the power to change how you feel inside. Shaken, tired and weak. I am not real. You made me real. I hear your thoughts call me."

"Little Bit, I like nothing better than being nothing. I used to enjoy moving about at ease, flying high with a bird's-view of above and below. You and all the other Bits brought me down to earth with a thud. You listened to the Virus and gave me a name. I still get to take off now and then, but you keep calling me back."

Fear continued. "I am not the fear when you think something will fall on your head or when you need to jump out of the way. You know what to do to keep yourself safe. Little Bit, look inside yourself again. Look inside your heart and remember. Your heart is so full of love for others. Now fill it with love for yourself. Make your heart so filled with love that it spills out everywhere and to everyone. You are Love and loved. As you do that, please send me love too. That's right, to me, Fear. I would like to be set free. No doubt you will call me back, but please set me free as soon as you can. Remember, I am only what you make me."

Little Bit felt light and unable to stop smiling.

The hot air balloon landed. As Little Bit was being called to jump into the balloon's basket, Little Bit was feeling excited now and looking forward to lift-off. Especially when there was a whisper in Little Bit's ear.

"Come on, let's go flying so we can get a bird's-eye view of above and below. Let's have some fun."

Little Bit laughed because Little Bit felt so light and could have floated even without a balloon.

7
A Little Bit of Faith

Little Bit was at the beach at last, walking along the sand, enjoying the water rushing over Little Bit's feet. Little Bit breathed in deeply while taking in the creative patterns the sun made on the water. Everything seemed big and open at the beach.

Little Bit always felt excited when gathering with other Bits, enjoying walking among the trees, taking time in the park and drinking in the colours of the circus. And now Little Bit knew the liberating sensation of floating high above everything in a hot air balloon.

All these wonderful places, but if Little Bit could only have one favourite place, it would be here at the beach. Being at the beach never failed to lift Little Bits spirits, and Little Bit always left the beach feeling calm and refreshed.

Little Bit felt comforted by the sound of the waves breaking. So tuned into the sound, it took a while to hear voices calling out for Little Bit to wait for them. Little Bit stopped, amazed to see so many other Bits running along trying to catch up. Little Bit found a smooth rock to sit on and waited.

Some Bits were out of breath, some fit Bits not so much, when they made it to where Little Bit waited.

Little Bit was happy yet amazed to see them all, even though they were all trying to talk at once.

At last there was a pause when Little Bit asked, "What are you all doing here?"

One of the fit Bits that was hardly out of breath stepped forward saying, "Little Bit, we wanted to spend some time with you. We see how bright you have become. Even when you struggle nothing seems to dim your Light or the Love we see and feel coming from you."

For a moment, Little Bit was so quiet, not knowing where to start or what to say. Little Bit always wanted to help others. Perhaps this was a way.

Finally, Little Bit spoke.

"Some time ago, someone really close to me told me to look at the word FAITH and to have Faith."

"Faith in what?" all the Bits asked.

Little Bit smiled and continued. 'Faith in yourself. If you look at the word and how it's spelled, you might understand. As that someone explained, FADE AWAY IDEAS THAT HINDER your belief in yourself. Fade away what isn't true for you, though it may be for someone else. Where do your ideas come from? Are they yours or someone else's? Do they help you or hinder you from believing in yourself? There are some that help and some that don't. That's for you to choose."

Some Bits were smiling, some nodding their heads and some mumbling.

Watching this, Little Bit went on. "Believing in yourself doesn't mean you deny how you feel. Even an unhappy thought needs to see the light of day. The Virus made us afraid to be different. Made us fear those unlike ourselves. It made us afraid to reach out and touch another in case we became more infected. Made us pretend not to care. Now we know it didn't make us do anything. We let it happen. It's like a big game we have all been playing. We have been confused for so long by what isn't real, we lost sight of how we can Trust what is Real."

Little Bit smiled. "We can be part of changing the game. Some will wish to create a new game based on remembering our original loving self and our connection to a creative source which goes by whatever name you give it—Creator, Source, God, Nature, Energy or Universe. Some will watch the new game unfolding, but keep playing the old game with fearful connections. That is ok too. Being thoughtful and compassionate will help you with others that play the old games."

A very tall Bit stepped forward and said, "Thanks Little Bit, but what really works for you?" Tall Bit was getting agitated with swinging arms and saying, "Little Bit, we see you when you are sad or angry or troubled and it's as though a mountain is in front of you. Yet you take off and run up it, stop at the top, look around, then choose a more joyous path down the other side and you are always smiling."

Tall Bit said, "I have even heard you laughing to yourself."

"Yes, Tall Bit," Little Bit said. "I laughed at myself because for a moment I forgot, then looked at how crazy I was being. It didn't matter whether it was feeling hurt from unmet expectations, rushing around, making mistakes, being thoughtless, sad, impatient or fearful. When I remembered, I forgave myself because it was me doing it. And in that moment of forgiveness I would feel joy rushing back in and laugh. We can be so funny. The Faith I practice and the more I forgive myself; these dark moments get shorter and shorter. Then, as more Love fills my heart, the more I have to share. In your mind, the mountaintop is a good place to go. Up high you can look down and see the light in those dark moments. The light never disappears; you simply choose it."

A Short Bit pushed to the front and said to Little Bit, "There's something else, Little Bit. What is it?"

Little Bit thought maybe enough had been said. Realising the Bits wanted to hear more, Little Bit continued.

"When you focus on finding the light in the dark, you understand what's been happening, especially your role. Like the duck peddling away, you understand what you are moving through. With that understanding comes Awareness. Go back to the idea of the mountaintop. You'll realise what took you there and that Awareness will help you tune into the voices inside of you that help you. You then stay aware of what you say to yourself and others. Awareness will always help you know when something feels right for you and when something doesn't."

Short Bit was thankful about knowing more, then thought of something Little Bit said some time ago.

"Little Bit, I just remembered a story you told me about meeting a Water Diviner when you were out walking. How the Diviner's rods would come together in the presence of water. Do you remember what you told me? What you understood and learned from that meeting?"

Nodding, Little Bit said, "Why yes, it helped me understand that we are all DIVINE. Like the Water Diviner seeking water, we are seeking Truth and the paths through Life that are best for each of us. Which is us simply being our Divine Selves."

'Divine', thought the Bits. And as they all made space inside themselves for this new thought, there was such a feeling of joyous relief spreading through all the Bits. They were Divine, and they were seekers of Truth. This new Thought connected them all.

Little Bit looked over the heads of all the Bits, and they all turned to see where Little Bit was looking. What they saw was the shimmering presence of the Wise Bit, Thoughtful Bit, The Clown and Fear.

Then they heard them say, "Little Bit, finish the story and tell them Who is Little Bit?"

With a smile, Little Bit said, "You are Little Bit... and You... and You... and You... In fact, everyone reading this, You are Little Bit. We are all Little Bits. At any one time a Bit of this and Bit of that coming together, connecting ready to support other Bits to work in harmony to become our whole selves."

Welcome the Little Bits in each of you that listens, questions, discerns and knows how perfectly ok you are.

Find that favourite place where you can take time to enjoy being you. Remember to take calm deep breaths.

Take a moment right now to smile a smile so big it is felt in and by every Bit of You.

About the Artist

Lennie Robson was born in Newcastle NSW in 1948 having a typical 50's upbringing, women at home men did the work. Though Lennie lived in an industrial suburb she gravitated towards colour. At fourteen she commenced her first job where she met her first BEST friend who she regards as still exerting an influence in her life today. She taught Lennie about the simplicity of Japanese art and design through her Ikibana arrangements. Since then Lennie has loved how colour can create a mood or even a feeling.

Being born after the second World War, for married women it wasn't the DONE thing to even think of working, let alone move into artistic circles.

After raising two children, in her later years Lennie began to express herself through painting. She loves how colour moves in water and hopes to spend the rest of her life exploring this phenomenon.

About the Author

Patricia Lovell has three grown sons two stepsons and six grandchildren and lives with her husband in the Lake Macquarie area NSW, Australia.

Patricia has been a Remedial Massage Therapist since 1988.She is an intuitive facilitator of healing light energy and brings her healing touch to every modality she practices and is particularly passionate about Craniosacral therapy, Voice Dialogue and Genome DNA and Stem Cell healing.

One of Patricia's many hats is that of a teacher and has written and taught professionally accredited courses. Many therapists have benefited from her sharing of knowledge and openness in her teachings.

Over a period of many years Patricia has also taught meditation, personal and spiritual development. Courses she devised include 'Breathing Your Way to Peace'-'Tools For Moving Forward'-'Building Self -Esteem' to name a few.

Healing the Inner Child within herself and others has been one of Patricia's life goals and feels she is now becoming drawn to support, with her words, children and young adults through the increasing anxiety and uncertainty of our times.

She yearns for her vision for our future adults and world leaders to become a reality. Visualising them as loving, kind, compassionate, strong yet flexible and focused on the higher good of all.

Copyright © Patricia Lovell 2020

First published by Patricia Lovell
with guidance of Karen Mc Dermott

Edited by: Dannielle Line

All rights reserved. No part of this publication may be reproduced, stored in a retrieval system, or transmitted in any form or by any mean, electronic, mechanical, photocopying, recording or otherwise, without the prior written permission of the publisher.

National Library of Australia
Cataloguing in-Publication entry

Patricia Lovell, Little Bit
ISBN: 978-0-6488499-1-9 (sc)
ISBN: 237-0-0008087-8-3 (hc)
ISBN: 978-0-6489519-4-0 (e)

The National Library of Australia CIP info:
1. Juvenile fiction - general. 2. Juvenile fiction - inspiration

Cover and interior illustrations by Lennie Robson

Printed and bound on sustainable paper in partnership with
Lightning Source AU Pty Ltd.

www.ingramcontent.com/pod-product-compliance
Lightning Source LLC
Chambersburg PA
CBHW041500010526
44107CB00044B/1520